Wheels Around Aberdeen

by
Alan Brotchie

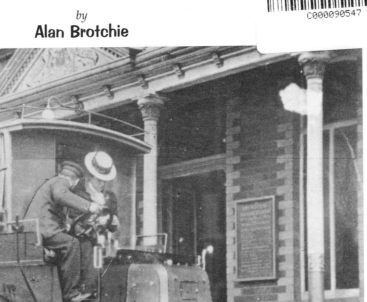

A moment frozen in time at the Bathing Station *c.*1900. This little Milnes–Daimler bus was operated by the Motor Service Co. Ltd. and probably had its wagonette-style body fitted by James Stirling of Hamilton in Lanarkshire. A fare of 2d was charged for the trip from Market Street, a not inconsiderable amount then, which probably meant that the service was more often taken for its novelty value than as a regular means of transport. Stirling was involved in the establishment of similar pioneering motorbus operations from 1898 onwards, including short-lived services in Edinburgh, Ayr, Falkirk, Rothesay and Blackpool to name just a few. However, the early vehicles employed were found to be liable to breakdown and hence reliability was poor. Note the coat of arms of the city above the door of the building. More familiarly known in later days as simply 'the baths', the Bathing Station closed in July 1972 and was demolished shortly thereafter.

ISBN 1 84033 248 4

The publishers regret that they cannot supply
copies of any pictures featured in this book.

HAMILTON PLACE, ABERDEEN.

Hamilton Place (at King's Gate) is one of Aberdeen's many handsome suburban streets. This view looks eastwards from Whitehall Road. The street was laid out in the 1880s and named after Professor Robert Hamilton – an eccentric academic who had an observatory constructed on Castlehill for his own use. Hamilton Place is notable for the exuberance of design expressed by architects Pirie & Clyne, whose work can be seen not only here but through much of the mid-Victorian development of the city. It is a delight to take the time to examine the often whimsical detailing of many of these homes. The handsome pram on the left is entirely suited to these surroundings.

INTRODUCTION

Until 2000, when Inverness was elevated to city status as part of the millennium celebrations (along with Brighton and Wolverhampton), Aberdeen was the farthest-flung of Britain's cities and had an unsurprising air of isolation. In addition to its geographical remoteness, the sense of isolation was exacerbated by poor road links, a situation that has only been remedied to some extent in the last twenty years with completion of the A90 dual carriageway (the former A94) to Stonehaven and the south. This remoteness was felt even more acutely in the years before the arrival of the main railway connection, and has always given Aberdeen and its hinterland a special quality and feeling of independence. Since its earliest days the city's total lack of mineral resources for fuel required a mercantile fleet which formed an adjunct to the large North Sea fishing fleet. In view of the lack of coal to be found locally, it is ironic that Aberdeen has now become the centre of Britain's North Sea oil industry.

Aside from the road system, which developed in the most rudimentary fashion from the Middle Ages, the first local manifestation of the transport revolution was seen in the construction of the eighteen mile Aberdeenshire Canal from Waterloo Quay to Inverurie in 1805. This served to open up the agricultural hinterland, allowing produce to be transported to the city and beyond (although it was not until 1834 that the canal was connected through to the harbour). One of the earliest regular passenger services was operated on the canal, which was eventually purchased and incorporated into the next major transport development – the railway.

Stagecoach travel on the turnpike road network was not highly developed between Aberdeen and the south, with most long-distance journeying being undertaken by sea until the arrival of a railway line. On 16 March 1850 the Aberdeen Railway arrived from the south to a temporary terminus at Ferryhill, thus providing the city with its first link to the national rail network. The subsequent extension of this line to the city centre was made via a series of arches forming a viaduct, and the Aberdeen Railway eventually went on to form part of the main line owned by the Caledonian Railway.

What could perhaps be thought of as Aberdeen's own railway was the Great North of Scotland which served the north-east corner of the country from 1854 running from Aberdeen to Huntly, Keith and Peterhead. The linking of the Caledonian Railway and the GNSR through the Den Burn valley in the 1860s caused almost as much anguish in Aberdeen as had the construction of the railway line through Edinburgh's Princes Street Gardens. It is difficult to imagine if either of these schemes would progress today in the face of the resistance of the conservationists. At the 1923 railway grouping the Caledonian became the major Scottish part of the LMS Railway while the GNSR became a minor part of the LNER.

Following well-established precedents throughout Britain, horse bus services gave way to horse-drawn trams in the 1870s, then the electric trams which replaced them were in turn replaced by buses in the 1950s/60s. The trams were started in the city – as in other places – by a private limited company, became successful and were then purchased by the municipality. Electrification followed, providing a constant demand for the local (municipally-owned) power station. The Aberdeen Suburban Tramways Company, a separate undertaking, provided extensions to the Corporation lines to Bankhead and Bieldside. In the late 1920s these two lines succumbed to bus competition, a harbinger of the fate to befall the remainder of the tram network 30 years later.

For many years a feature of the local transport scene was the prudent use of redundant vehicles as stores etc. on farms. Old tramcars, railway coaches and vans provided inexpensive lodgings for chickens and livestock. One happy consequence of this 'eye for a bargain' was the use of the bodies of the two small tramcars from the Cruden Bay Hotel electric tramway as summerhouses, one of which can be seen, lovingly restored, at the Grampian Transport Museum at Alford, Aberdeenshire. Another local idiosyncrasy was the continued use of steam lorries long after they had disappeared from the streets of most other cities – again ensuring that examples were preserved for posterity.

In this selection I have tried to present a varied cross-section of what was Aberdeen's extremely complex and varied transport scene, hopefully conjuring up memories of days not so long past. My thanks are extended on this occasion to Robert Grieves and Alan Simpson for their much appreciated assistance.

Photographed in 1897, this may well be the first 'horseless carriage' to have been seen on the streets of Aberdeen. Probably a Benz, it was owned by local entrepreneur William Jackson (wearing the boater), who in addition to inventing tea-processing machinery also dabbled in automotive design. Seated next to him is P. N. Shinnie – of the well-known coachbuilding family – who's firm may have been responsible for this vehicle's coachwork. On its first run, to Kincardine O'Neil, it was said that 'many near catastrophes occurred, causing Shinnie to exclaim "It's as though every horse in Deeside was warned of its new competitor" '. The photograph was taken outside Thorngrove, Jackson's home on Great Western Road.

Not content with owning Aberdeen's first motor car, William Jackson also managed to acquire the first registration number when issue commenced by the city as required by the Motor Car Act of 1903. This photograph dates from the following year and shows Jackson's 25 hp Maudslay landaulet on the left, with another similar vehicle on the right (RS 144) and a small single-cylinder Rover (RS 161) between them. In the early years of the last century the Maudslay was a popular car in the north-east, probably because Sir Charles Forbes of Newe in Strathdon was chairman of the company. When two-letter registration numbers were exhausted and a prefix letter system commenced, the combination ARS was avoided to prevent offending local sensibilities. However, in the fullness of time ERS – which is, of course, the local pronunciation of the word deemed to be offensive – *was* issued!   **5**

A busy Victorian scene looking north from Union Street up St Nicholas Street under the unwavering gaze of that lady herself. Queen Victoria's statue was unveiled here in 1893, but in 1964 was relocated to Queen's Cross, from where she looks west towards Balmoral. The tram line along St Nicholas Street, the start of Great Northern Road, was one of the first in Aberdeen, opening as far as Powis Terrace on 31 August 1874. Operated by the city's Aberdeen District Tramways Company, the vehicle in the centre of the picture is horse tram Kittybrewster No. 5, with a longitudinal (or knifeboard) seat on the top deck. Each service had its own dedicated batch of cars which were painted a particular colour; in this case red. All horse trams purchased by the tramways company after 1883 were built locally by R. & J. Shinnie, whose nameplate can still be found on former horse tram No. 1, now displayed at the Grampian Transport Museum at Alford.

Horse cars on the Rosemount circular service were painted white, as illustrated in this view of two cars on Rosemount Place at the end of South Mount Street. Car No. 4 is another product of the R. & J. Shinnie coachbuilding workshop. From 26 August 1898 the horse trams passed from private ownership into the control of Aberdeen Corporation. The company was paid £104,000 for the entire operation, producing £15 for each £10 share. Considering that for several years the shareholders had received a dividend, this was a reasonable return on their confidence in the enterprise. This carefully posed view is from an old three-inch square glass magic lantern slide – curly-brimmed bowler hats were definitely in fashion for the well dressed 'loon' at the time!

The Corporation electrified and extended the tramways, creating a compact and highly successful operation which – through the profits generated – contributed significantly to the relief of the rates. Here three trams, en route to Bridge of Don and possibly on a private hire, pause at the south end of King Street long enough to have their photograph taken. The fine millinery worn by the female passengers – who outnumber by a large percentage the men on the trip – is worthy of particular note. The inside saloons of the cars are empty, with all passengers assembled outside for the photograph. Like the top decks, the drivers' platforms were completely open to the elements at this stage, and while covers for passengers on upper decks were provided soon afterwards, drivers had no protection whatsoever for many more years. When a form of windscreen was eventually provided, drivers then complained about the resultant draughts!

Two electric tram routes extending from the Corporation's network beyond the city boundaries were constructed and operated by the independent Aberdeen Suburban Tramways Company. Both operated over the Corporation's lines into the city centre. One line – the 'Deeside' – ran from Castle Street to Bieldside; the other – the 'Donside' – from St Nicholas Street to Bankhead. This postcard shows a tram at Cults on the Deeside route c.1906. Initially owning only six trams (making it by far the smallest Scottish tramway) the company never operated more than eleven. As a result of intense

bus competition and deteriorating track, their tram operation ceased in 1927.

In June 1914 the Suburban Company bought three of these double deck buses, which were probably intended for a route from Bieldside to Culter. They were Tilling–Stevens petrol electric vehicles and probably represented the greatest single investment made by the company during its existence. The service to Culter was an early casualty of the First World War, which saw the buses put to use ferrying wounded service personnel to and from local hospitals. They probably escaped being drafted to aid the war effort in France by virtue of their non-standard engines and transmission. This picture of RS-X-29 was taken at Woodend Hospital. While RS was the registration letter combination for Aberdeen, it would seem that a separate RS-X series was also maintained for 'other' types of vehicle. This arrangement continued until 1921, when the first Corporation bus was registered RS-X-135, before subsequently becoming the less distinctive RS 3711.

To overcome manpower shortages during the First World War, so-called 'conductrettes' were recruited, with this record made of the first intake in June 1915. Most interestingly this particular postcard was sent to a prisoner of war in Germany and has been overstamped 'Geprüft. Kommandantur Gef-Lager Dülmen' (Examined. Commander's headquarters Prison-Camp Dulmen). The message reads 'Dear Hugh, This will give you an idea of what like Ab is getting woman doing man's work – do you recognise Poppy' – a poignant message from a difficult time. By the end of the war, 123 of the total number of 130 conductors were women. In addition there were five women acting as drivers and one female inspector.

Aberdeen's Female Car Conductors—Full Staff, June 19, 1915.

An Aberdeen conductress (as the conductrettes were better-known) with her driver and car 81 at Mannofield. This particular tram was delivered in 1914, just before the outbreak of war, and was designed on the 'pay as you enter' patented principle with entry by the platform at the rear and exit at the front. This feature was done away with in 1923 (which gives a 'latest' date for this photograph) and the car ran until 1950. Note that the driver now has a modicum of protection with a folding windscreen invented by the Corporation Tramways Manager, R. S. Pilcher.

This winter scene at King Street tram depot gives some indication of the privations which tram drivers could be subjected to – just imagine how it was before rudimentary windscreens were provided. Here one of the later streamlined cars sits at the depot entrance. These particular cars had difficulty in operating in these conditions, and it was not unknown for them to be taken out of service and the older 'Standard' type put on in their place.

The suitability of the smooth steel tram rails for other forms of transport is graphically illustrated here, and carters such as this one routinely steered their vehicles onto the rails to make their progress along the cobbled streets easier. Taken at the west end of Union Street, this photograph is packed with interest, from the message boy and his bike on the right to the cart on the left complete with wicker laundry baskets. This belonged to the Aberdeen Steam Laundry Company which advised that they were also 'Dyers, French Cleaners and Carpet Beaters'. In the centre of the picture is the tower of Gilcomston (South) Church, one of only two sandstone buildings on Union Street. The soft stone deteriorated to such an extent that the spire had to be demolished in the late 1980s and was then completely rebuilt.

Aberdeen Corporation tramcar No. 104 photographed at Mannofield terminus in 1939. There is no other road traffic apart from two cycles and a motorbike. During the war most of the gold lining which is seen here on the vehicle was discontinued. Cars on the Great Western Road route had a brown route colour band below the top deck windows. Prior to 1927 the tracks of the Aberdeen Suburban Tramways Company continued off to the left for a further three miles to Bieldside. Aberdeen's last tram ran on 3 May 1958.

The Aberdeen 'County' registration letters were SA. Dating from 1907, SA 311 was one of the very earliest double deck buses to be built and operated by the Great North of Scotland Railway Company. They pioneered several rural routes into areas not served directly by the railway, and notices on the board at Schoolhill station, right, refer to services to Dyce, Newburgh, Echt, Midmar, Waterton and Cluny. The 28 hp Milnes–Daimler had a body built at the railway company's Inverurie workshops, with seating for ten passengers inside plus a further eighteen outside. This photograph was taken at Rosemount Viaduct, with a backdrop summarised by generations of Aberdonians as 'Education, Salvation and Damnation' plus, if one includes the station, 'Transportation'. The other three building referred to are of course the library, church and theatre.

Early motor vehicles – such as the Great North's bus, seen on the facing page, took a heavy toll on the water-bound macadam roads of the time. This charming posed period piece came from a collection of Aberdeenshire views and is said to have been taken on the South Deeside road. Unfortunately the precise location has not been identified. The Aveling steam road roller has a two-part front roller, which was a normal feature, although the two sections were not usually separated in the manner of this machine. The horses have waited patiently during the camera's long exposure, but the roller driver has moved and consequently appears as a blur!

Salmon fishing on the River Dee in the early years of the twentieth century. The wheeled contrivance on the bank was employed to wind in nets (hopefully filled with fish), and is obviously portable. Three salmon fishings were owned by the Harbour Commissioners, and in 1950 were valued at £50,000, with the capacity to produce up to 200 fish daily in season. The arches of the sixteenth century Bridge of Dee can be seen upstream. It has stood the test of time remarkably well, albeit aided by two reconstructions: one in 1720 and a second 120 years later. During the latter rebuild it was widened from twelve feet to its present 40-foot width, the upstream-facing stones being taken down then reinstated so that the widened bridge retained its original appearance. Behind the old house on the right there was a boating pond which was popular in winter for skating.

A First World War photograph of the power generating room at the old barracks on Castlehill, vacated by the army in 1935. The reverse of the picture provides considerable information which renders the scene identifiable. 'This little wonder makes the light and cooks with electricity the boiler does all the heating of barracks when the turbine is running the exhaust steam is sent round the barracks so it does two jobs quite economical – what. It is situated in the old gas plant room in North Casements.' After the army left the building was used for housing and was demolished in 1965. The eighteen-storey Marischal Court flats were then built on the site.

Edwardian cyclists, such as the one gentleman and group of ladies seen here, would probably not have appreciated Union Street's granite setts; they would have felt every joint as they cycled up the street! The ladies' attire would seem to be entirely inappropriate for cycling today but was the height of fashion and decorum then – even to the broad-brimmed hats. Indeed it is noteworthy that, unlike modern times, every individual in the picture, without exception, is wearing a hat. While Union Street may run in a straight line, it is far from level, as these cyclists would have been well able to confirm. By this time tram 45 had acquired a top deck cover for the benefit of passengers, but the driver is still completely at the mercy of the elements.

Albyn Place, possibly photographed during the sedate Edwardian rush hour, with another of Aberdeen's well-dressed lady cyclists again sporting impressive headgear. Albyn Place was developed from 1820 on James Skene's Rubislaw estate. His Edinburgh town house was in the New Town, in Albyn Place, and it was on the New Town that he modelled his new development – even to the extent of giving it the same name. The buildings of the High School for Girls are on the right.

The North British Railway was one of several railway companies which combined to operate Aberdeen's Joint station in Guild Street. In PR terms the North British had an inspired policy with regard to the naming of their passenger train locomotives, most of which had a Scottish theme. Of the eight new express engines built in 1906, the very first was *Aberdonian*, while the third, *Bon Accord*, also honoured the city. *Aberdonian* was exhibited to the press on 2 July of that year, briefly painted in this grey livery so as to more clearly show its lines in photographs. It ran for most of its existence on the east coast main line express services to Dundee and Edinburgh, and was withdrawn in September 1933.

Railway Station, Culter.

A 1907 photograph taken at Culter station on the Deeside line of the Great North of Scotland Railway. These 'Subbie' (Suburban) trains, as they were known, were introduced in 1894 to cater for burgeoning commuter traffic. From Culter 21 minutes was allowed for the seven miles into the Joint station – and this had to include no fewer than eight stops at intermediate stations. Competition from the Aberdeen Suburban Tramways Company arrived in June 1904, but the rail service held its own until the 1920s when the bus services which saw off the trams took much of the rail passenger traffic also. The last of the true 'Subbie' trains ran in April 1937, although Culter did retain a passenger service until 28 February 1966. It then closed, a victim of the infamous axe of Dr Beeching.

In its original form, Aberdeen's Joint station in Guild Street became notorious for its cramped and claustrophobic conditions. The platforms at the south end were used by the trains of three different railway companies, the Caledonian, the Great North of Scotland and the North British (which only gained access by way of the rails of the Caledonian Railway after construction of the bridge over the Tay at Dundee and agreement for through running to Aberdeen). This view shows on the left a Caledonian express bound for the south, and to the right a Great North train for the Deeside route to Ballater.

The busy Joint station was reconstructed (without closing) between 1907 and 1914. This photograph was taken in 1914 as the last remaining arches of the old roof were removed. Some of the working practices would give today's Health and Safety Executive nightmares.

In 1923 the North British Railway became part of the much larger London & North Eastern Railway. This view dates from just after then, and shows the departure of the 9.50 a.m. passenger express for Edinburgh, which was reached in just over three hours. Today's diesels take on average two and a half hours – not a vast improvement over that schedule. The leading locomotive is the *Highland Chief*, assisted by *Kenilworth* which appears to be doing most of the work. On the right are two former Caledonian Railway locomotives, and behind the trains on the left is the Corporation electricity generating station. The express usually contained coaches for Glasgow which were uncoupled at Dalmeny then worked direct to Queen Street station.

The Great North of Scotland Railway built their main locomotive sheds and workshops at Kittybrewster, but moved the workshops to a much more spacious site at Inverurie in 1902. Kittybrewster then remained as the main depot for locomotives working to the north. On 15 September 1933 this 'stranger in the camp' was photographed there. Bearing the number 7222, it was fitted with cowcatchers of distinctly North American appearance for working on the unfenced Fraserburgh to St Combs Light Railway. The small engine was built in 1907 by the Great Eastern Railway and was one of a large number of similar locomotives generally to be found working around London. Renumbered 67164, it lasted until August 1951.

Railway traffic to and from Aberdeen's docks was handled by small locomotives of which this one, built for the Great North of Scotland Railway, was typical. It dated from 1915 when the Harbour Authority first allowed locomotives to be used instead of horses, and was photographed at the docks on 9 August 1949. Following eleven years further service, it was scrapped in April 1960. Despite the fact that most of these quayside tracks were effectively on the road there was never a requirement for these locomotives to have their moving parts enclosed. Most locos working in such circumstances were required to have the motion covered, as indeed did those operated near here by the Aberdeen gasworks.

The 'Murcar trainie' was one of Aberdeen's transport curiosities. This three-foot gauge line ran from near Bridge of Don to Murcar Golf Club, using the petrol railcar illustrated. It was built (or rebuilt) locally by T. C. Smith – the radiator is mounted on the roof! Caddies were expected to occupy the platform at the rear, but over 30 passengers could be accommodated inside the car. A second railcar was purchased in 1932 and operations continued until the end of June 1950. After closure the body of the older car became the ladies' caddy car store, the gentlemen members getting the newer vehicle for their caddy cars.

In sharp contrast to today's heavy traffic, there is only one vehicle to be seen in this view of Beechgrove Terrace, probably dating from 1906. The terrace is now best known as the home of the BBC's local television (originally radio) studios, and as the location of the renowned *Beechgrove Garden* series and its cast of characters. Tram 34 was supplied in 1903 as an open-topper, but acquired its top deck cover in 1905. This distinguished street of solid granite homes was recently described as comprising 'Italianate small mansion houses, somewhat baronial hybrids'. Note the decorative gas street lamp with its 'Tramway Station' sign – not for Aberdonians a mere tram stop!

Horse lorries, bicycles and other traffic pass the weigh-house, which formerly sat at the north-west corner of the Upper Dock. Guild Street led off to the left giving access to the passenger and goods stations, hence this was always an area of intense activity. Market Street, ahead, leads up to Union Street. Construction of the street commenced in 1840, and it was so named for the New Market which was formerly situated on its east side. Rebuilt after a fire in 1882, the market building was demolished in 1971, with the two basement floors of the British Home Stores structure built on its site given over as replacement accommodation for markets.

Handcarts are to the fore in this photograph of George Street, with, most surprisingly, not a tram in sight. This entire area at the junction with Schoolhill and Upper Kirkgate was changed forever with the construction of the Bon Accord Centre in 1989–90, transforming George Street into a cul-de-sac. Named to commemorate King George III, it was laid out in the same year as Market Street, 1840, and was designed to provide a new, direct route to the harbour and market from the Inverurie direction. The junction was controlled by a points policeman who had to keep his wits about him, as there was insufficient space for him to stand between the tram tracks when two trams were passing.

URQUHART ROAD (LOOKING WEST), ABERDEEN

Urquhart Road looking west from Urquhart Street towards King Street. By the time this photograph was taken (probably in the early 1920s), motor vehicles had started to become more commonplace. This development was Aberdeen Council's first municipal housing project, built in 1897–99 for slum clearance. Although without gardens, the three-storey granite tenements did possess that civilising influence and communal meeting point, the 'stairheid lavie'. Named after the first chairman of the City of Aberdeen Land Association (CALA), the street's main claim to fame was its boisterous Hogmanay celebration. At Paterson's corner shop bills advertise 'Free peppermint rock' (what's the catch?). The shop on this corner has since been reconstructed as a dwelling-house, but most of the other corners of this individualistic street have retained their shops.

Market Street and The Harbour, Aberdeen   "Adelphi Series"

South Market Street was – and remains – a major centre of activity in the heart of the city. Traffic to and from the fish market, coal for bunkering the many steam trawlers of Aberdeen's fleet, and much, much more combined to give it its unique character. Here tram 35 is threading a careful track to St Fittick's Road, terminus of the Torry route. Torry was the last area of the city to be reached by trams, in 1903, and also lost them earlier than elsewhere – in 1931. The Tramway Department wanted to replace this delaying length of single track with a double line, but the Harbour Trust refused, hastening the decision to abandon the Torry route.

Aberdeen harbour is still one of Britain's busiest, now full of vessels serving the North Sea oil and gas industry. It has long been one of the country's largest harbours, with its earliest charter going back to the reign of King David I of Scotland in 1136. Timber imports from the Baltic formed a major part of the trade, as did imports of coal. On the day this photograph was taken only one horse lorry was to be seen, while the unloading of the cargo was being undertaken by two old mobile steam cranes.

Paddle wheels are in evidence here as the tug *Fairweather* waits to take control of the newly launched SS *Intaba* from the Hall, Russell shipyard in 1910. By today's standards the *Intaba* is not a large vessel, but at 386 feet she was at that time the largest the yard had built. She was owned by John T. Rennie & Sons, and was generally to be found on the East Africa run. Hall, Russell was the largest of several local shipbuilders and was staffed by up to 1,000 hands at peak employment. Many trawlers for the local fishing fleet were constructed at the yard, as was the very first UK oil rig supply vessel. Site space restrictions limited the dimensions of vessels which could be fabricated, and after a short existence as Aberdeen Shipbuilders the yard closed in 1988.

HEATHER DAY AT ABERDEEN - SCENE IN DUTHIE PARK
HOLMES' SERIES

Many fund-raising events were held during the First World War to provide 'comforts' for troops on active service at the front and to support the war effort in other ways. In August 1915 a 'Heather Day' was held at Duthie Park, in this case to raise money for Aberdeen's Royal Infirmary. This group are exchanging their bunches of heather for donations ultimately destined for the Infirmary. The original Aberdeen Infirmary dated back to 1739, but long before this in 1492 Britain's first medical school had been founded at King's College. Based at what became a cramped site at Woolmanhill, the foundation stone of a new complex at Foresterhill was laid in 1936 by the then Prince of Wales (later King Edward VIII).

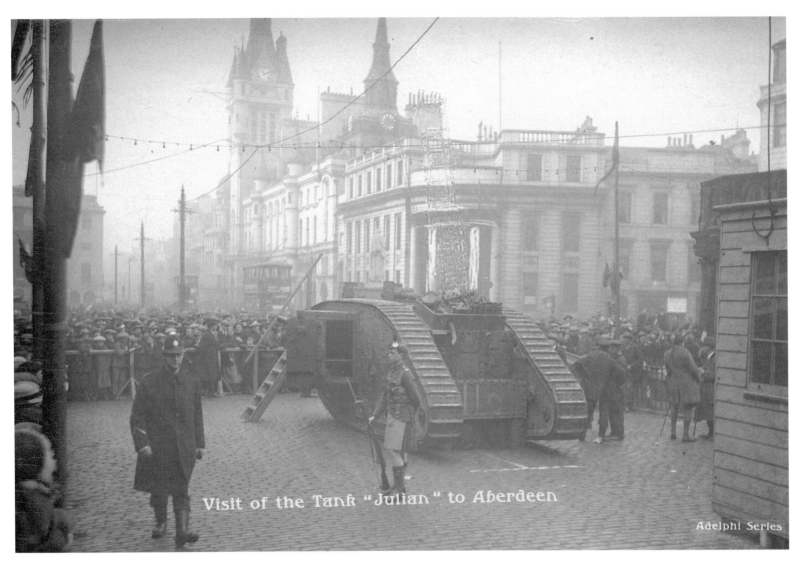

Visit of the Tank "Julian" to Aberdeen

Adelphi Series

In 1917 funds were raised by the tank *Julian* touring round the country. Used for the first time in the First World War, tanks such as *Julian* were seen at the time as the epitome of modern warfare and excited great interest. This tank was not driven from place to place on its tour, but was transported by rail on a special wagon.

Aberdeen was for many years a centre of steam wagon operation, the economy and longevity of these vehicles endearing them to many local transport undertakings. This Standard Sentinel was registered in Lanarkshire, where many of them were constructed. The group was photographed at Wm. Reith's Kennerty Farm *c*.1920. The names and jobs of most present are known, and give a fascinating glimpse of farm employment then.

Back row (left to right): W. Kane (little cattleman), W. Keith (orraman), J. McKenzie (orraman), C. Middleton (third horse man), R. Barron (second horse man), W. Webster (first horse man)

Front row: D. McKenzie (head cattleman), Q. Mitchell Jnr. (groom's son), unknown (milk boy), two drivers, names unknown, Q. Mitchell (groom).

Another operator of Sentinel steam wagons was the Aberdeen Coal & Shipping Company which took delivery of this seven ton Super Sentinel on 1 December 1924 and named it *Tiger*. It had a sister, *Lion*, and with a following wind these two big cats could reach 30 mph. *Tiger* was used without interruption for over 40 years, delivering coal throughout Aberdeenshire. During this extended period it was driven solely by Alexander Burnett. In 1966 it was purchased for restoration.

The Sentinel certainly was popular with Aberdeen coal merchants. This one, RS 6540, was operated by Ellis & McHardy of 18 Regent Quay, with such refinements as pneumatic tyres and a driver's windscreen. One or two of these vehicles were operated at Aberdeen harbour during the Suez fuel crisis of 1957, shunting wagons on the railway.

This well laden but front-heavy looking Albion lorry was owned by the Aberdeen carriers Will & Co. of Summerfield Terrace, off King Street. The undertaking was taken over by the nationalising British Road Services in the late 1940s. Used regularly between Aberdeen and Inverness, it is here seen in the latter city – in Bank Street in front of the Dr Black Memorial Hall on the banks of the River Ness.

A Leyland Comet lorry of 1958 being loaded with lime for agricultural purposes from a coaster at Aberdeen harbour. The makeshift work platform should raise eyebrows today.

A Bedford Luton furniture van with the over-cab extension with which most removals vehicles were fitted, photographed in Weigh-house Square off Regent Square. The weigh house was demolished in 1885 to allow construction of the Harbour Board offices. Founded in 1498, the Shore Porters Society must surely have the longest existence of any single commercial organisation in Scotland.

This unusual design of bus, an AEC 'Q' type, registration RG 4539, was purchased by the Rover Company, one of Aberdeen's independent bus operators. Rover was one of the largest of these independents and was thus named because the proprietor enjoyed travel, having been to America (and returned to Aberdeen!). The route operated was from King's Gate to Torry, thus competing with the Torry trams and hastening their abandonment. With effect from 14 November 1935 the Rover Company was purchased by Aberdeen Corporation and this bus then became No. 104, lasting until 1948. It is seen here loading in Union Terrace.

The Corporation ultimately owned thirteen of the 'Q' type, of which two were formerly with Rover. No. 23 (RG 5623) was fitted with bodywork by local firm William Walker's Coachworks of Ashgrove Road. Use of such local employers became a contentious political matter as they did not always submit the cheapest tender. However, the council supported local industry whenever possible and in the years from 1929 to 1936 over 60 bus bodies were purchased from Walker. Castle Street, as is well illustrated here in 1938, was then the hub of the city's transport services.

The 'Ace' bus service operated from Aberdeen to Elgin and Mr A. Laing, who owned it, made use of Walter Kennedy's garage here at 70 John Street. Being carefully guided back into the narrow entrance is a De Dion Bouton, RS 7962. The proximity of the gas lamp standard must have had an effect on the care which is being exercised. John Street was also home to the stables of Wordie's the carters, and long caravans of horse lorries could be seen setting off from here each morning for the day's work.

These two 1938 Daimler COG6 double deck buses were photographed at the Union Street/Market Street junction. That on the left, with a Weyman body, was exhibited at the Scottish Motor Show, while the one on the right was bodied locally by William Walker Ltd.

This looks like a Le Mans start, but is more likely to be 'lousing time' at Hall, Russell's. The location is Trinity Quay at the foot of Market Street. Bus 138 is a Daimler with Duple bodywork, one of only four vehicles released to the Corporation under the war conditions of 1943, built with a 'Utility' body and wooden seats. Given more comfortable seating in 1948/9, these four Duples remained in service until 1965.

Some idea of the popularity of the facilities at the beach in the 1930s is given by this view taken from the Broad Hill. There are few motor cars in evidence, and most of those on the esplanade and around the bandstand will have come by tram. Trams from Castle Street reached the beach by a private right of way which cut eastwards across the Links to terminate here – right in the centre of all the activity. They arrived and left every few minutes.

As in many continental cities, part of the holiday experience was a trip by horse-drawn coach. In Aberdeen this service seems to have been one of the losses of the Second World War.

Day tours and mystery tours to local and more distant attractions were also a major part of any holiday, and also appealed to local people. Aberdeen was (and is) a popular holiday destination, and 'The Silver City with the Golden Sands' is a timeless description. This tour bus was run by William Ledingham's Tours (operating as FF&F – as seen on the side of the vehicle). FF&F had originated as one of the competing independent bus companies of the 1920s. The original proprietor was John Bonnar, a wholesale grocer and it was said that FF&F stood for 'Fresh Fruit and Fowls' (or Fish). This vehicle is an AEC with Seagull bodywork by Burlingham of Blackpool.

ROYAL FLYING CORPS. BIPLANE ON ABERDEEN LINKS

"Adelphi Series"

Here crowds have been drawn to the Links by the lure of heavier-than-air flying machines, including this biplane, one of the first to be owned by the Royal Flying Corps. Until January 1919 the Scottish Aircraft Factory at Forbesfield built Avro biplanes, thereby making a major contribution to the success of First World War aviation. Dyce was used as an RAF base until 1946, and thereafter, until the arrival of the oil industry in the late 1960s, was treated by BEA as rather a backwater. The situation changed dramatically after that when it became the busiest heliport in Britain and one of the busiest airports.